WELCOME TO THE WORLD OF DAD JOKES!

Dad jokes are those groan-inducing, eye-roll-worthy puns and one-liners that dads (and some moms, uncles, and grandparents) love to tell. They're often characterized by their corniness, simplicity, and predictability, but that's exactly what makes them so endearing. Dad jokes aren't about being genuinely funny in the traditional sense; they're about creating a sense of lightheartedness and camaraderie through shared silliness.

In this book, I'll guide you through the art of using dad jokes to your advantage. Whether you're looking to lighten the mood in a tense situation, break the ice with a new acquaintance, or simply entertain your family and friends, dad jokes are the perfect tool. With a little practice and the right timing, you'll have everyone groaning and giggling along with you in no time.

Now, you may have heard some of these jokes before – and that's perfectly okay! Dad jokes are timeless classics that never fail to bring a smile to people's faces, even if they've heard them a hundred times before. So sit back, relax, and prepare to enjoy a hearty dose of dad humor.

After all, life's too short not to appreciate a good pun, no matter how "bad" it may be!

I HAD AN OUT-OF-BODY
EXPERIENCE LAST WEEK.

I WAS BESIDE
MYSELF.

◈◈◈

PEOPLE SAY THEY PICK
THEIR NOSES...

I FEEL LIKE I WAS JUST
BORN WITH MINE.

◈◈◈

Q: WHAT DID THE OCEAN
SAY TO THE SHORE?

A: NOTHING, IT JUST
WAVED.

I WENT TO A HALLOWEEN PARTY AS THE JOKER, BUT I COULDN'T SEE ANYONE THERE.

IT WAS A DARK KNIGHT.

———◇◇———

Q: WHY DID THE BANK ROBBER TAKE A BATH?

A: HE WANTED TO MAKE A CLEAN GETAWAY!

———◇◇———

Q: WHAT DID ONE TOILET SAY TO THE OTHER TOILET?

A: YOU LOOK FLUSHED.

Q: HOW DO YOU TELL IF A GRAVEYARD IS POPULAR?

A: PEOPLE ARE DYING TO GET IN THERE

SON: HOW DO I LOOK?

DAD: WITH YOUR EYES!

Q: WHAT DO YOU CALL A COW WITH NO LEGS?

A: GROUND BEEF.

I USED TO HAVE A JOB AT THE CALENDAR FACTORY, BUT I GOT CANNED BECAUSE I TOOK A COUPLE OF DAYS OFF.

Q: WHERE DOES BATMAN GO TO THE BATHROOM?

A: THE BAT-ROOM.

Q: WHAT DID THE RED LIGHT SAY TO THE GREEN LIGHT?

A: DON'T LOOK, I'M CHANGING.

Q: HOW DO YOU IMPRESS A FEMALE BAKER?

A: BRING HER FLOURS.

Q: WHERE DO COWS HANG THEIR PAINTINGS?

A: IN THE MOO-SEUM.

Q: WHAT DID THE POLICEMAN SAY TO HIS BELLY BUTTON?

A: YOU'RE UNDER A VEST!

Q: WHY DID THE COOKIE GO TO THE EMERGENCY ROOM?

A: BECAUSE HE FELT CRUMMY!

———◇◇———

Q: WHY DID YOUR MOM THROW THE CLOCK OUT THE WINDOW?

A: SHE WANTED TO SEE TIME FLY!

———◇◇———

Q: WHAT DO YOU CALL FAKE NOODLE?

A: AN IMPASTA!

Q: WHAT DO YOU CALL A BEAR WITH NO TEETH?

A: A GUMMY BEAR!

Q: WHERE DO SNOWMEN KEEP THEIR MONEY?

A: IN THEIR SNOW BANK!

Q: WHY DID THE CHICKEN GET A PENALTY?

A: FOR FOWL PLAY.

MY BACK GOES OUT MORE THAN I DO!

I DON'T LIKE RUSSIAN DOLLS.

THEY'RE SO FULL OF THEMSELVES.

Q: WHY DID DAD PUT HIS MONEY IN THE FREEZER?

A: HE WANTED COLD HARD CASH!

Q: WHAT DO YOU CALL A PIG WITH THREE EYES?

A: A PIIIG!

Q: WHAT KIND OF MUSIC DO CHIROPRACTORS LIKE?

A: HIP POP!

Q: WHY SHOULDN'T YOU WRITE WITH A BROKEN PENCIL?

A: BECAUSE IT'S POINTLESS!

Q: HOW DO YOU GET A BABY ALIEN TO SLEEP?

A: YOU ROCKET!

Q: HOW DO YOU MAKE A TISSUE DANCE?

A: YOU PUT A LITTLE BOOGEY IN IT!

THE PROBLEM ISN'T THAT OBESITY RUNS IN YOUR FAMILY...

THE ACTUAL PROBLEM IS THAT NO ONE RUNS IN YOUR FAMILY.

Q: WHAT DO YOU CALL A SLEEPING BULL?

A: A BULLDOZER!

Q: WHY DON'T CANNIBALS EAT CLOWNS?

A: THEY TASTE FUNNY!

I'M SO OLD, ALL I BUY IS SYMPATHY CARDS.

Q: WHAT BISCUIT DOES A SHORT PERSON LIKE?

A: SHORTBREAD!

I'M SO OLD, I REMEMBER WHEN PHONE CORDS WERE KINKY AND SEX WASN'T.

I WAS GOING TO TELL YOU A HILARIOUS TIME-TRAVEL JOKE...

BUT YOU DIDN'T LIKE IT.

Q: WHY WOULDN'T THE SHRIMP SHARE HIS TREASURE?

A: BECAUSE HE WAS A LITTLE SHELLFISH.

Q: WHAT DO YOU CALL A SKETCHY ITALIAN NEIGHBORHOOD?

A: THE SPAGHETTO

Q: WHAT DO YOU CALL A BEAR WITH NO EARS?

A: B.

I KNOW A TON OF JOKES
ABOUT UNEMPLOYED
PEOPLE...

BUT NONE OF THEM WORK.

———————◇◇◇———————

Q: WHAT DID THE JUDGE
SAY WHEN THE SKUNK
WALKED INTO
THE COURT ROOM?

A: ODOR IN THE COURT!

———————◇◇◇———————

I'M AT AN AGE WHERE IF IT
WEREN'T FOR FUNERALS, I
WOULDN'T HAVE AN
SOCIAL LIFE AT ALL.

———————◇◇◇———————

I'M SO OLD, MY BIRTHDAY CAKE LOOKS LIKE A WILDFIRE!

DAD, CAN YOU PUT MY SHOES ON?

NO, THEY WON'T FIT ME.

Q: WHAT DOES A BABY COMPUTER CALL HIS FATHER?

A: DATA!

Q: WHAT DO YOU HAVE IN MY SIZE?

A: THE FREIGHT ELEVATOR.

Q: WHY DID THE ORANGE STOP HALFWAY UP THE HILL?

A: HE RAN OUT OF JUICE.

Q: WHY IS IT ALWAYS COLD IN STADIUMS?

A: THEY'RE FULL OF FANS!

Q: WHAT'S WORSE THAN FINDING A WORM IN YOUR APPLE?

A: FINDING HALF A WORM!

Q: HOW MANY TICKLES DOES IT TAKE TO MAKE AN OCTOPUS LAUGH?

A: TEN-TICKLES.

I ONCE HAD A DOG WITH NO LEGS.

EVERY DAY I WOULD TAKE HIM OUT FOR A DRAG.

Q: WHAT DO YOU GET WHEN YOU DROP A PIANO DOWN A COAL SHAFT?

A: A FLAT MINOR.

Q: WHAT IS THE LOUDEST PET YOU CAN GET?

A: A TRUMPET!

19

Q: WHAT DO YOU CALL A MAN WITH A SEAGULL ON HIS HEAD?

A: CLIFF

Q: WHY DID THE BANANA GO TO THE DOCTOR?

A: HE WASN'T PEELING WELL!

Q: WHAT DO YOU CALL A DOG THAT CAN DO MAGIC?

A: A LABRACADABRADOR!

Q: WHAT'S BROWN AND STICKY?

A: A STICK!

Q: WHAT'S THE DIFFERENCE BETWEEN A JEWELER AND A PRISON WARDEN?

A: ONE SELLS WATCHES AND THE OTHER WATCHES CELLS.

Q: WHAT DO YOU CALL AN ALLIGATOR IN A VEST?

A: AN INVESTIGATOR!

Q: WHAT LIES ON THE SEABED AND SHIVERS?

A: A NERVOUS WRECK!

I USED TO HAVE A JOB COLLECTING LEAVES...

I WAS RAKING IT IN!

Q: WHAT'S THE BEST DAY TO GO TO THE BEACH?

A: SUNDAY, OF COURSE!

Q: WHAT HAPPENS IF A FROG PARKS ILLEGALLY?

A: THEY GET TOAD.

Q: WHY SHOULDN'T YOU PLAY CARDS IN THE JUNGLE?

A: THERE'S TOO MANY CHEETAHS!

Q: HOW DO YOU MAKE TOAST IN THE JUNGLE?

A: PUT YOUR BREAD UNDER

Q: HOW DO HENS CHEER FOR THEIR TEAM?

A: THEY EGG THEM ON!

Q: WHY DO CRABS NEVER GIVE TO CHARITY?

A: THEY'RE SHELLFISH

Q: WHY DID THE MAN WITH ONE HAND CROSS THE ROAD?

A: TO GET TO THE SECOND-HAND SHOP.

Q: WHY DO BAKERS WORK SO HARD?

A: THEY KNEAD THE DOUGH.

Q: WHY COULDN'T YOU HEAR THE PTERODACTYL GO TO THE BATHROOM?

A: BECAUSE THE P WAS SILENT!

Q: WHY DO BEES HUM?

A: BECAUSE THEY DON'T KNOW THE WORDS!

SON: DAD, WHY HAVEN'T YOU TALKED TO MOM AT ALL THIS WEEK?

DAD: WELL, SON, I DON'T LIKE TO INTERRUPT HER.

Q: WHAT BOW CAN'T BE TIED?

A: A RAINBOW!

Q: WHAT'S THE DIFFERENCE BETWEEN A HIPPO AND A ZIPPO?

A: ONE'S REALLY HEAVY AND THE OTHER IS A LITTLE LIGHTER!

Q: HOW DOES A ONE ARMED MAN TIE HIS SHOES?

A: SINGLE HANDEDLY.

DID YOU HEAR ABOUT THE CIRCUS FIRE?

IT WAS IN TENTS!

I NAMED MY DOGS ROLEX AND TIMEX.

THEY'RE MY WATCH DOGS!

Q: HOW DOES NASA ORGANIZE A PARTY?

A: THEY PLANET!

Q: WHAT DO YOU GET IF YOU CROSS THE ATLANTIC WITH THE TITANIC?

A: JUST OVER HALFWAY.

Q: WHAT DO YOU CALL A DEER WITH NO EYES?

A: NO IDEA.

Q: WHAT DO YOU CALL A PONY WITH A SORE THROAT?

A: A LITTLE HOARSE.

Q: WHO'S THE MOST WANTED MAN IN THE OCEAN?

A: AL CAPRAWN.

I DON'T KNOW WHY TREES MAKE ME SO NERVOUS...

I GUESS BECAUSE THEY'RE SO SHADY.

Q: WHAT KIND OF FISH BAIT DO LIBRARIANS USE?

A: BOOKWORMS.

Q: WHY IS ENGLAND THE WETTEST COUNTRY?

A: THE QUEEN REIGNED

27

Q: WHAT DO YOU CALL AN ELEPHANT THAT DOESN'T MATTER?

A: IRRELEPHANT.

Q: WHAT AWARD DID THE KNOCK-KNOCK JOKE WRITER WIN?

A: THE NO-BELL PRIZE.

Q: WHAT DO YOU CALL A PERSON WITH NO BODY AND NO NOSE?

A: NOBODY KNOWS.

Q: WHAT'S BLUE AND SQUARE?

A: AN ORANGE IS DISGUISE.

Q: WHY CAN'T AN EAR BE 12 INCHES LONG?

A: BECAUSE THEN IT WOULD BE A FOOT.

I ORDERED A CHICKEN AND AN EGG ON AMAZON...

I'LL LET YOU KNOW WHICH COMES FIRST!

Q: WHAT DID THE DAD SPIDER SAY TO THE BABY SPIDER?

A: YOU SPEND TOO MUCH TIME ON THE WEB!

Q: WOULD GLASS COFFINS SELL WELL?

A: REMAINS TO BE SEEN...

Q: WHO IS THE SECOND-MOST WANTED MAN IN THE OCEAN?

A: JACK THE KIPPER.

I JUST WATCHED A DOCUMENTARY ABOUT THE LIFE OF BEAVERS.

IT WAS THE BEST DAM THING I'VE EVER SEEN!

Q: WHAT HAS ONE HEAD, ONE FOOT, AND FOUR LEGS?

A: A BED

Q: HOW CAN YOU TELL IF AN ANT IS A BOY OR A GIRL?

A: THEY'RE ALL GIRLS, OTHERWISE THEY'D BE UNCLES.

Q: WHAT DO SEA MONSTERS EAT FOR DINNER?

A: FISH & SHIPS

Q: WANT TO HEAR A JOKE ABOUT PAPER?

A: NEVER MIND, IT'S TEARABLE.

Q: WHAT DID THE MERMAID WEAR TO MATH CLASS?

A: AN ALGAE-BRA.

Q: HOW DO YOU CATCH A FISH IN THE DARK?

A: WITH GLOW-WORMS!

Q: WHY DID THE OCTOPUS BEAT THE SHARK IN A FIGHT?

A: BECAUSE HE WAS WELL ARMED.

Q: HOW MANY APPLES GROW ON TREES?

A: ALL OF THEM.

Q: WHAT GOES SNAP, CRACKLE?

A: TWO RICE KRISPIES.

WE MIGHT GO SNORKELING THIS WEEKEND, BUT I'M NOT HOLDING MY BREATH.

Q: WHY ARE SKELETONS SO CALM?

A: NOTHING CAN GET UNDER THEIR SKIN.

———◇◇———

Q: WHY DID ROGER GO OUT WITH A PRUNE?

A: HE COULDN'T FIND A DATE!

———◇◇———

Q: WHY AREN'T KOALAS BEARS?

A: THEY DON'T MEET THE KOALAFICATIONS.

———◇◇———

Q: WHAT'S A COW'S FAVORITE CEREAL?

A: MOO-SLI.

Q: WHY DID THE BUNNY GO TO THE HOSPITAL?

A: BECAUSE HE NEEDED A HOP-ERATION!

Q: WHY DID THE FLORIST SELL HIS SHOP?

A: HE COULD SEE NO FUCHSIA IN IT.

Q: WHAT'S ORANGE AND SOUNDS LIKE A PARROT?

A: A CARROT.

Q: WHAT'S A FOOT LONG AND SLIPPERY?

A: A SLIPPER.

Q: WHEN DOES A JOKE TURN INTO A DAD JOKE?

A: WHEN IT BECOMES APPARENT.

Q: WHAT DO YOU CALL A FLY WITHOUT WINGS?

A: A WALK

Q: WHY DID THE BELT GET ARRESTED?

A: HE HELD UP A PAIR OF PANTS.

Q: WHERE DOES THE KING KEEP HIS ARMIES?

A: IN HIS SLEEVIES.

Q: WHAT DID THE SHOE SAY TO THE CONFUSED HAT?

A: YOU GO ON AHEAD.

Q: WHY IS PETER PAN ALWAYS FLYING?

A: HE NEVERLANDS.

Q: WHY DO YOU NEVER SEE ELEPHANTS HIDING IN TREES?

A: BECAUSE THEY'RE SO GOOD AT IT.

MY WIFE TOLD ME TO STOP ACTING LIKE A FLAMINGO.

I HAD TO PUT MY FOOT DOWN.

Q: WHY DID THE COWBOY GET A WIENER DOG?

A: HE WANTED TO GET A LONG

Q: WHAT'S THE TALLEST BUILDING IN THE WORLD?

A: THE LIBRARY, IT HAS THE MOST STORIES.

Q: WHAT'S THE BEST TIME OF DAY?

A: 6:30, HANDS DOWN.

Q: WHY DON'T SKELETONS EVER GO TRICK OR TREATING?

A: BECAUSE THEY HAVE NO BODY

37

Q: WHAT'S THE BEST TIME TO GO TO THE DENTIST?

A: TOOTH HURT-Y!

Q: DOES ANYONE NEED AN ARK?

A: I NOAH GUY.

Q: WHAT HAS FOUR WHEELS AND FLIES?

A: A GARBAGE TRUCK.

I TRIED WATCHING THE NEVER-ENDING STORY...

COULDN'T FINISH IT.

Q: WHY DID THE MAN DECIDE TO SELL HIS VACUUM?

A: IT WAS JUST COLLECTING DUST.

Q: CAN ONE BIRD MAKE A PUN?

A: NO, BUT TOUCAN.

Q: WHAT DID THE DRUMMER NAME HIS TWIN DAUGHTERS?

A: ANNA 1, ANNA 2!

Q: WHAT DO YOU CALL CHEESE THAT ISN'T YOURS?

A: NACHO CHEESE

Q: WHEN IS A DOOR NOT A DOOR?

A: WHEN IT'S AJAR.

Q: WHY CAN'T YOU CAN'T TRUST ATOMS?

A: THEY MAKE UP EVERYTHING.

Q: WHAT SOUND DOES A WITCHES CAR MAKE?

A: BROOM BROOM!

Q: WHY DID THE COFFEE FILE A POLICE REPORT?

A: IT GOT MUGGED.

Q: WHAT DO SPRINTERS EAT BEFORE A RACE?

A: NOTHING, THEY FAST.

Q: WHY CAN'T THE BANK KEEP A SECRET?

A: IT HAS TOO MANY TELLERS.

Q: WHY ARE FROGS SO HAPPY?

A: THEY EAT WHATEVER BUGS THEM.

Q: WHY DO GEOLOGISTS HATE THEIR JOBS?

A: THEY GET TAKEN FOR GRANITE.

41

Q: WHY DID THE PAINTING GO TO JAIL?

A: IT WAS FRAMED!

I LOVE TELLING DAD JOKES.

SOMETIMES HE EVEN LAUGHS.

Q: WHY ARE ELEVATOR JOKES SO GOOD?

A: THEY WORK ON MANY LEVELS

Q: WHEN DOES A TAILOR NEED TO GO ON VACATION?

A: WHEN THEY SEEM STRESSED.

Q: WANT TO HEAR A JOKE ABOUT CATS?

A: JUST KITTEN!

Q: WHAT HAS ONE HORN AND GIVES MILK?

A: A MILK TRUCK.

Q: WHAT STATE HS THE MOST STREETS?

A: RHODE ISLAND.

Q: HOW DO YOU MAKE AN EGG ROLL?

A: JUST GIVE IT A LITTLE PUSH.

Q: WHERE DO FRUITS GO ON VACATION?

A: PEAR-IS!

Q: WHY WAS THE CAT ASKED TO LEAVE THE COMPUTER STORE?

A: HE WOULDN'T STOP PLAYING WITH THE MOUSE!

Q: WHAT'S WORSE THAN WHEN IT'S RAINING CATS AND DOGS?

A: HAILING TAXIS.

MY EXTRA WINTER WEIGHT IS FINALLY GONE.

NOW, I HAVE SPRING ROLLS.

Q: WHY DO DADS TAKE AN EXTRA PAIR OF SOCKS WHEN THEY GO GOLFING?

A: IN CASE THEY GET A HOLE IN ONE.

◇◇◇

Q: WHAT IS THE BEST THING ABOUT LIVING IN SWITZERLAND?

A: WELL, THE FLAG IS A BIG PLUS.

◇◇◇

A HAM SANDWICH WALKS INTO A BAR AND ORDERS A BEER.

THE BARTENDER SAYS, "SORRY WE DON'T SERVE FOOD HERE."

Q: WHAT DID THE COMPUTER DO FOR HIS LUNCH BREAK?

A: HAD A BYTE.

———◇◇———

Q: WHY DON'T BANKS ALLOW KANGAROOS TO OPEN ACCOUNTS?

A: THEIR CHECKS ALWAYS BOUNCE!

———◇◇———

DID YOU HEAR ABOUT THE ATM THAT GOT ADDICTED TO MONEY?

IT SUFFERED FROM WITHDRAWALS.

———◇◇———

I USED TO HATE FACIAL HAIR, BUT THEN IT GREW ON ME.

MY HOTEL TRIED TO CHARGE ME $70 EXTRA FOR AIR CONDITIONING.

THAT WASN'T COOL.

Q: WHAT DO YOU CALL A SINGING LAPTOP?

A: A DELL.

IF TWO VEGANS GET IN A FIGHT, IS IT STILL CONSIDERED A BEEF?

Q: WHAT'S FORREST GUMP'S EMAIL PASSWORD?

A: ONEFORESTONE.

Q: WHY DO MELONS HAVE WEDDINGS?

A: BECAUSE THEY CANTALOUPE.

———◇◇———

Q: HOW DOES A BEE BRUSH ITS HAIR?

A: A HONEYCOMB

———◇◇———

A CHEESE FACTORY EXPLODED IN FRANCE.

DA BRIE IS EVERYWHERE!

———◇◇———

Q: WHAT DO YOU GET FROM A PAMPERED COW?

A: SPOILED MILK

Q: IF ATHLETES GET ATHLETE'S FOOT, WHAT DO ASTRONAUTS GET?

A: MISSILE TOE.

Q: WHAT DO YOU CALL A LAZY KANGAROO?

A: A POUCH POTATO.

Q: WHAT DO YOU CALL A FISH WITH TWO KNEES?

A: A TWO-KNEE FISH!

Q: WHY CAN'T YOU TELL A TACO A SECRET?

A: THEY TEND TO SPILL THE BEANS

WHENEVER I TRY TO EAT HEALTHY, A CHOCOLATE BAR LOOKS AT ME AND SNICKERS.

A BOOK FELL ON MY HEAD.

I ONLY HAVE MY SHELF TO BLAME.

Q: HOW DO YOU MAKE HOLY WATER?

A: YOU BOIL THE HELL OUT OF IT.

Q: WHAT DO YOU CALL TWO MONKEYS THAT SHARE AN AMAZON ACCOUNT?

A: PRIME MATES.

Q: WHERE DO MATH TEACHERS GO ON VACATION?

A: TIMES SQUARE.

Q: WHY DOES SNOOP DOGG ALWAYS CARRY AN UMBRELLA?

A: FO' DRIZZLE.

Q: WHAT DOES GARLIC DO WHEN IT GETS HOT?

A: IT TAKES ITS CLOVES OFF.

Q: CAN FEBRUARY MARCH?

A: NO, BUT APRIL MAY!

IF YOU SEE A CRIME AT AN APPLE STORE, DOES THAT MAKE YOU AN IWITNESS?

Q: WHERE DO BAD RAINBOWS GO?

A: PRISM, IT'S A LIGHT SENTENCE.

Q: WHAT DOES CORN SAY WHEN IT GETS A COMPLIMENT?

A: AW, SHUCKS!

Q: WHAT DO COMPUTERS EAT FOR SNACKS?

A: MICROCHIPS!

Q: HOW DO YOU PLAY LEAPFROG WITH A PORCUPINE?

A: VERY CAREFULLY.

Q: HOW DO SNAILS FIGHT?

A: THEY SLUG IT OUT!

Q: CAN A MATCH BOX?

A: NO, BUT A TIN CAN.

Q: WHAT DO YOU CALL A PILE OF CATS?

A: A MEOWTAIN.

ONE DAY I WAS IN THE PARK WONDERING WHY FRISBEES GET BIGGER...

THEN IT HIT ME.

Q: WHY DO OCEANS NEVER GO OUT OF STYLE?

A: THEY'RE ALWAYS CURRENT.

Q: WHAT DO YOU CALL A GIRL WHO JUST GOT BACK FROM THE BEACH?

A: SANDY.

Q: DID YOU HEAR ABOUT THE ITALIAN CHEF?

A: HE PASTA WAY.

Q: WHAT DO YOU CALL A MAN WHO CAN'T STAND?

A: NEIL.

Q: WHERE DO YOU TAKE A SICK BOAT?

A: TO THE DOCK.

Q: WHAT DID THE SCHIZOPHRENIC BOOKKEEPER SAY?

A: I HEAR INVOICES.

Q: HOW FUNNY ARE MOUNTAINS?

A: THEY'RE HILL AREAS.

Q: WHAT DID THE BABY CORN SAY TO THE MAMA CORN?

A: "WHERE'S POP CORN?"

Q: WHAT DOES A NUT SAY WHEN IT SNEEZES?

A: CASHEW!!

Q: HOW DOES A RANCHER KEEP TRACK OF HISCATTLE?

A: WITH A COW-CULATOR!

MY CREDIT CARD COMPANY JUST SENT ME ANOTHER CAMOUFLAGED BULL!

IT'S THE HIDDEN CHARGES YOU REALLY HAVE TO WATCH OUT FOR!

Q: WHY ARE GHOSTS SUCH BAD LIARS?

A: YOU CAN SEE RIGHT THROUGH THEM!

Q: WHAT DO YOU CALL A BEE WITH A QUIET BUZZ?

A: A MUMBLEBEE!

Q: WHAT DID THE ANGRY HEDGEHOG SAY TO ITS ENEMY?

A: "I'M GOING TO QUILL YOU!"

Q: WHAT DO CATS EAT FOR BREAKFAST?

A: MICE KRISPIES!

DID YOU HEAR ABOUT THE HUGE SALE ON CANOES?

IT WAS QUITE THE OAR DEAL!

◆◆

Q: WHEN THE SMOG LIFTS IN LOS ANGELES, WHAT HAPPENS?

A: UCLA.

◆◆

Q: WHERE DO ANIMALS GO WHEN THEY LOSE THEIR TAILS?

A: TO THE RETAIL STORE.

◆◆

Q: HOW DOES AN ESKIMO BUILD HIS HOUSE?

A: IGLOOS IT!

Q: WHEN IS A CAR NOT A CAR?

A: WHEN IT TURNS INTO THE GARAGE.

Q: WHAT DID THE MOUNTAIN CLIMBER NAME HIS SON?

A: CLIFF.

Q: WHY DO YOU GO TO BED?

A: THE BED WON'T COME TO

Q: WHY ARE FISH SO EASY TO WEIGH?

A: THEY HAVE THEIR OWN SCALES.

DID YOU HEAR ABOUT THE TWO GUYS WHO STOLE A CALENDAR?

THEY EACH GOT SIX MONTHS.

Q: WHAT DO VAMPIRES CROSS THE OCEAN IN?

A: BLOOD VESSELS.

Q: WHERE DO BABY GORILLAS SLEEP?

A: IN AN APE-RI-COT.

Q: HOW DO BILLBOARDS TALK?

A: SIGN LANGUAGE.

Q: WHY ARE ZOMBIES NEVER LONELY?

A: THEY CAN ALWAYS DIG UP NEW FRIENDS.

Q: WHY SHOULD YOU HOLD THE DOOR OPEN FOR A CLOWN?

A: IT'S A NICE JESTER.

Q: WHAT DO YOU CALL A WOMAN WITH ONE LEG SHORTER THAN THE OTHER?

A: EILEEN.

Q: HOW DO YOU SHOOT A KILLER BEE?

A: WITH A BEE-BEE GUN.

Q: WHERE DID THE COW TAKE HIS DATE?

A: THE MOOOOVIES!

Q: WHAT KIND OF UNDIES DO CLOUDS WEAR?

A: THUNDERWEAR.

Q: WHAT DID ONE SNOWMAN SAY TO THE OTHER SNOWMAN?

A: DO YOU SMELL CARROTS?

Q: WHY CAN'T TOWELS TELL SILLY JOKES?

A: THEY HAVE A DRY SENSE OF HUMOR.

Q: WHAT DID THE BEAVER SAY TO THE TREE?

A: IT'S BEEN NICE GNAWING YOU!

Q: WHAT HAS A BOTTOM AT THE TOP?

A: A LEG.

Q: WHAT'S MORE IMPRESSIVE THAN A TALKING DOG?

A: A SPELLING BEE!

Q: WHERE CAN YOU GET CHICKEN BROTH IN BULK?

A: THE STOCK MARKET.

Q: WHY DID THE CAT RUN FROM THE TREE?

A: BECAUSE OF ITS BARK!

Q: WHAT DO YOU CALL A SLEEPING NUN?

A: A ROAMIN' CATHOLIC.

Q: WHAT DID THE HORSE SAY WHEN HE FELL?

A: HELP! I'VE FALLEN AND I CAN'T GIDDY UP!

Q: WHAT DID THE OLD LAMP SAY TO ITS NEW LIGHT BULB?

A: YOU'VE GOT A BRIGHT FUTURE, KID!

Q: WHAT DO YOU CALL A FAT PSYCHIC?

A: A FOUR CHIN TELLER!

Q: WHAT IS SANTA'S FAVORITE MUSIC?

A: WRAP.

I'M NOT ADDICTED TO BRAKE FLUID...

I CAN STOP WHENEVER I WANT!

Q: WHAT DO YOU CALL A ROW OF PEOPLE LIFTING MOZZARELLA?

A: A CHEESY PICK UP LINE.

Q: WHY DID THE POOR MAN SELL YEAST?

A: TO RAISE SOME DOUGH.

Q: WHY DID THE PLUMBER QUIT HIS JOB?

A: IT WAS TOO DRAINING!

THE INVENTOR OF THE THROAT LOZENGE HAS DIED...

THERE WILL BE NO COFFIN AT HIS FUNERAL.

Q: WHAT KIND OF CARS DO SHEEP DRIVE?

A: LAMB-ORGHINIS.

Q: WHAT COLOR IS THE WIND?

A: BLEW.

Q: WHAT DID THE MOUSE SAY TO THE CAMERA?

A: CHEESE!

Q: WHY DID THE ASTRONAUT MOVE TO THE SUBURBS?

A: HE NEEDED MORE SPACE.

Q: WHAT DO YOU CALL A NOSY PEPPER?

A: JALAPENO BUSINESS!

Q: WHY DID THE GIRL SMEAR PEANUT BUTTER ON THE ROAD?

A: TO GO WITH THE TRAFFIC JAM!

Q: WHAT DO YOU CALL AN OWL THAT CAN DO MAGIC TRICKS?

A: HOOOOODINI

Q: WHAT DID WINNIE THE POOH SAY TO HIS AGENT?

A: SHOW ME THE HONEY!

RIP BOILED WATER...

YOU WILL BE MIST!

Q: WHY DIDN'T THE VAMPIRE ATTACK TAYLOR SWIFT?

A: SHE HAD BAD BLOOD.

Q: WHAT DID THE DAD CHIMNEY SAY TO THE SON CHIMNEY?

A: "YOU'RE TOO YOUNG TO SMOKE!"

Q: WHY DOES HUMPTY DUMPTY LOVE AUTUMN?

A: BECAUSE HUMPTY DUMPTY HAD A GREAT FALL.

Q: WHICH REINDEER LIKES TO CLEAN?

A: COMET.

DID YOU HEAR THAT ARNOLD SCHWARZENEGGER WILL BE DOING A MOVIE ABOUT CLASSICAL MUSIC?

HE'LL BE BACH.

Q: WHY DO COWS WEAR BELLS?

A: BECAUSE THEIR HORNS DON'T WORK!

Q: WHAT NAILS DO CARPENTERS HATE TO HIT?

A: FINGERNAILS.

I ATE A CLOCK YESTERDAY...

IT WAS VERY TIME CONSUMING.

Q: WHY SHOULD YOU NEVER IRON A FOUR LEAF CLOVER?

A: YOU NEVER WANT TO PRESS YOUR LUCK.

Q: WHAT DID THE BOY VOLCANO SAY TO THE GIRL VOLCANO?

A: I LAVA YOU!

Q: WHAT DO LAWYERS WEAR TO COURT?

A: LAWSUITS.

I WENT TO THE ZOO AND SAW A BAGUETTE IN A CAGE.

THE ZOOKEEPER SAID IT WAS BREAD IN CAPTIVITY!

Q: WHAT DO YOU CALL A PRETTY GHOST?

A: BOOTIFUL.

Q: WHY DID THE LION EAT THE TIGHT-ROPE WALKER?

A: HE WANTED A WELL BALANCED MEAL.

Q: WHAT DAY OF THE WEEK DO CHICKENS HIDE?

A: FRY-DAY.

Q: WHAT DID THE CROSS-EYED TEACHER SAY?

A: I CAN'T CONTROL MY PUPILS.

Q: WHAT DO YOU CALL BIRDS THAT STICK TOGETHER?

A: VEL-CROWS.

Q: HOW MANY LIPS DOES A FLOWER HAVE?

A: TU-LIPS.

Q: WHY ARE TEDDY BEARS NEVER HUNGRY?

A: THEY'RE ALWAYS STUFFED.

Q: WHAT DOES A TRICERATOPS SIT ON?

A: ITS TRICERABOTTOM.

Q: WHY DID THE CAN CRUSHER DECIDE TO QUIT HIS JOB?

A: BECAUSE IT WAS SODA-PRESSING.

---◇◇---

Q: WHERE DO SHEEP GO FOR A HAIRCUT?

A: THE BAA BAA SHOP.

---◇◇---

I HATE JOKES ABOUT GERMAN SAUSAGES...

THEY'RE THE WURST.

---◇◇---

Q: HOW ARE RELATIONSHIPS LIKE ALGEBRA?

A: SOMETIMES YOU LOOK AT YOUR X AND WONDER Y.

Q: WHERE DO YOU GO TO LEARN HOW TO MAKE ICE CREAM?

A: SUNDAE SCHOOL.

Q: WHY DON'T ANTS GET SICK?

A: THEY HAVE ANTY-BODIES.

SOME GUY JUST HIT ME IN THE FACE WITH A CHEESE WHEEL.

HOW DAIRY!

Q: WHAT DO YOU CALL A DEAD FLY?

A: A FLEW.

Q: HOW DO YOU FIND WILL SMITH IN THE SNOW?

A: YOU LOOK FOR FRESH PRINTS.

Q: WHAT'S THE MOST MUSICAL PART OF THE CHICKEN?

A: THE DRUM STICK.

I USED TO BE ADDICTED TO THE HOKEY POKEY...

BUT THEN I TURNED MYSELF AROUND.

Q: IS WHAT KEY DO COWS SING?

A: BEEF FLAT.

Q: WHAT DO YOU CALL A BEE THAT IS ALWAYS COMPLAINING?

A: A GRUMBLE BEE.

Q: WHY DO FISH LIVE IN SALT WATER?

A: PEPPER WOULD MAKE THEM SNEEZE!

Q: WHY DO COWS HAVE HOOVES INSTEAD OF FEET?

A: BECAUSE THEY LACTOSE.

Q: WHY ARE VAMPIRES SO EASY TO FOOL?

A: BECAUSE THEY'RE SUCKERS!

Q: WHY DID THE GIRL HIT HER BIRTHDAY CAKE WITH A HAMMER?

A: IT WAS A POUND CAKE.

---◆◆◆---

Q: HOW DO YOU GET A COUNTRY GIRL'S ATTENTION?

A: A TRACTOR.

---◆◆◆---

Q: WHAT DID AUNT JEMIMA SAY WHEN SHE RAN OUT OF PANCAKES?

A: "HOW WAFFLE!"

---◆◆◆---

Q: WHAT KIND OF BUG TELLS TIME?

A: A CLOCK-ROACH!

Q: WHAT DO YOU CALL A RABBIT COVERED IN FLEAS?

A: BUGS BUNNY.

Q: HOW DO YOU STOP A BEAR FROM CHARGING?

A: TAKE AWAY HIS CREDIT CARDS!

Q: ARE ELEPHANTS ALWAYS POOR?

A: THEY WORK FOR PEANUTS.

Q: HOW DO YOU FIND THE OLDEST RABBIT?

A: LOOK FOR A GRAY HARE.

Q: WHAT DO YOU CALL SOMEONE WHO IMMIGRATED TO SWEDEN?

A: ARTIFICIAL SWEDENER.

Q: WHERE DOES A HAMSTER GO FOR SPRING BREAK?

A: HAMSTERDAM.

I'VE BEEN TELLING EVERYONE THE BENEFITS OF EATING DRIED GRAPES.

I'M ALL ABOUT RAISIN AWARENESS!

Q: WHAT DO YOU CALL TWO FAT PEOPLE HAVING A TALK?

A: A HEAVY DISCUSSION.

Q: WHAT NOISE DOES A 747 MAKE WHEN IT BOUNCES?

A: BOEING, BOEING, BOEING.

Q: WHAT DID THE DUCK SAY TO THE BARTENDER?

A: PUT IT ON MY BILL.

Q: WHAT DO YOU GET WHEN YOU CROSS A SNAKE AND A PIE?

A: A PIE-THON.

Q: WHY CAN'T EGGS TELL JOKES?

A: THEY'D CRACK THEMSELVES UP!

Q: WHAT IS A HAPPY COWBOY'S FAVORITE CANDY?

A: JOLLY RANCHERS.

Q: WHAT DO YOU CALL A COW DIVA?

A: DAIRY QUEEN

Q: WHY DID THE TOMATO BLUSH?

A: IT SAW THE SALAD DRESSING.

Q: WHAT'S THE BEST SNACK TO EAT DURING A SCARY MOVIE?

A: I SCREAM.

Q: WHAT DO YOU CALL SHAVING CRAZY SHEEP?

A: SHEER MADNESS.

Q: WHAT DO YOU CALL AN EXPLODING MONKEY?

A: A BABOOM!

Q: HOW MUCH ROOM IS NEEDED FOR FUNGI TO GROW?

A: AS MUSHROOM AS POSSIBLE.

Q: WHERE DO RABBITS EAT FOR BREAKFAST?

A: IHOP.

Q: WHERE DO COWS GO ON VACATION?

A: MOO ZEALAND.

Q: WHAT DO YOU CALL THE NEW GIRL WORKING AT THE BANK?

A: NUTELLA.

Q: WHY DID THE ELEPHANTS GET KICKED OUT OF THE POOL PARTY?

A: THEY KEPT DROPPING THEIR TRUNKS!

Q: HOW DO YOU FIX A BROKEN PUMPKIN?

A: WITH A PUMPKIN PATCH!

———◇◇◇———

Q: WHAT IS THE PRETZEL'S FAVORITE DANCE?

A: THE TWIST.

———◇◇◇———

Q: WHERE DOES SPAGHETTI GO TO DANCE?

A: THE MEATBALL.

———◇◇◇———

DID YOU HEAR ABOUT THE CHAMELEON WHO COULDN'T CHANGE HIS COLORS?

HE HAD A REPTILE DYSFUNCTION.

Q: WHY CAN'T ORPHANS GO ON SCHOOL FIELD TRIPS?

A: NO PARENT SIGNATURES.

Q: WHAT HAS TWO BUTTS AND KILLS PEOPLE?

A: AN ASSASSIN.

Q: "DAD, ARE YOU ALRIGHT?"

A: "NO, I'M HALF LEFT."

Q: WHY DO SCUBA DIVERS FALL BACKWARDS INTO THE WATER?

A: BECAUSE IF THEY FELL FORWARDS, THEY'D STILL BE IN THE BOAT.

Q: WHY IS MILK THE FASTEST LIQUID ON EARTH?

A: IT'S PASTEURIZED BEFORE YOU EVEN

Q: WHY CAN'T YOU USE 'BEEF STEW' AS A PASSWORD?

A: IT'S NOT STROGANOFF.

Q: WHAT DO YOU CALL AN ALMOND IN A SPACESUIT?

A: AN ASTRONUT.

DID YOU HEAR ABOUT THE KID WHO CUT HIMSELF ON THE CHEESE?

IT WAS SHARP CHEDDAR.87

THERE'S A NEW TYPE OF BROOM OUT. HAVE YOU HEARD ABOUT IT?

IT'S SWEEPING THE NATION!

Q: WHY DID THE GIRL THROW BUTTER OUT THE WINDOW?

A: SHE WANTED TO SEE A BUTTERFLY!

Q: WHAT DID THE DA TOMATO SAY TO THE BABY TOMATO?

A: CATCH UP!

Q: WHAT KIND OF KEY CAN OPEN A BANANA?

A: A MONKEY.

Q: WHAT DOES A BANANA SAY WHEN IT ANSWERS THE PHONE?

A: YELLOW?

Q: WHY AREN'T ORPHANS GOOD AT BASEBALL?

A: THEY CAN'T FIND HOME.

DID YOU HEAR HOW THEY CAUGHT THE FAMOUS PRODUCE THIEF?

HE STOPPED TO TAKE A LEEK.

DID YOU SEE THE MOVIE ABOUT THE HOT DOG?

IT WAS AN OSCAR WIENER.

Q: WHAT'S THE DIFFERENCE BETWEEN A CAT AND A FROG?

A: A CAT HAS NINE LIVES AND A FROG CROAKS EVERY NIGHT.

Q: HOW DO YOU MAKE FRUIT PUNCH?

A: GIVE THEM BOXING GLOVES.

Q: WHAT KIND OF TEA IS HARD TO SWALLOW?

A: REALITY.

Q: WHY DID THE BEE GO TO THE DOCTOR?

A: HE HAD HIVES.

Q: HOW DO YOU FIX A BROKEN PIZZA?

A: TOMATO PASTE.

Q: WHAT KIND OF SHOES DOES A THIEF WEAR?

A: SNEAKERS.

Q: WHAT IS A GHOST'S FAVORITE PIE?

A: BOO BERRY.

Q: WHY DID THE SNACK CROSS THE ROAD?

A: TO GET TO THE OTHER SSSSSIDE.

91

Q: WHAT'S THE BEST WAY TO SNEAK CANDY INTO THE MOVIES?

A: HAVE A FEW TWIX UP YOUR SLEEVE!

◆◇◆

DID YOU HEAR ABOUT THE GUY WHO GOT GAS FOR $7.59?

HE ATE AT TACO BELL.

◆◇◆

Q: WHAT DO YOU CALL A STACK OF 52 PIECES OF BREAD?

A: A DECK OF CARBS.

◆◇◆

Q: WHAT DO YOU CALL A SMALL MOM?

A: A MINIMUM.

Q: WHY DOES KEEPING TROPICAL FISH IN YOUR HOME REDUCE STRESS AND ANXIETY?

A: BECAUSE OF THE INDOOR FINS.

Q: WHY WAS THE MATH BOOK SO SAD?

A: IT HAD A LOT OF PROBLEMS.

Q: WHY DID THE BLONDE STARE AT THE ORANGE JUICE CONTAINER?

A: IT SAID CONCENTRATE!

YOUR DAD WENT TO A SEAFOOD PARTY LAST WEEK... HE PULLED A MUSSEL.

MY BOSS TOLD ME TO HAVE A GOOD DAY...

SO I WENT HOME!

Q: WHY DID THE CAR GET A FLAT TIRE?

A: THERE WAS A FORK IN THE ROAD!

Q: WANT TO HEAR A JOKE ABOUT CONSTRUCTION?

A: I'M STILL WORKING ON IT.

I WROTE A SONG ALL ABOUT TORTILLAS.

ACTUALLY, IT'S MORE OF A WRAP!

Q: WHAT DO YOU CALL A COLD PUPPY?

A: A CHILI DOG!

I GOT CARDED AT A LIQUOR STORE AND MY BLOCKBUSTER CARD ACCIDENTALLY FELL OUT...

THE CASHIER SAID "NEVER MIND!"

Q: WHAT DO YOU CALL IT WHEN BATMAN SKIPS CHURCH?

A: CHRISTIAN BALE.

Q: HOW DO YOU KEEP A SKUNK FROM SMELLING?

A: HOLD ITS NOSE.

95

Q: HOW DID THE CITRUS GET TO THE PROM?

A: IN A LEMONZEEN!

Q: KNOW WHY GRANDPARENTS AND GRANDCHILDREN GET ALONG SO WELL?

A: A COMMON ENEMY.

Q: HOW DO TREES GET ONLINE?

A: THEY JUST LOG ON.

Q: WHY WAS THE COW SUCH A HEARTTHROB ON THE FARM?

A: HE WAS A S-MOOOO-TH

Q: WHAT KIND OF AWARD DOES THE WORLD'S TOP DENTIST GET?

A: A LITTLE PLAQUE.

I PUT YOUR GRANDMA ON SPEED DIAL THE OTHER DAY.

I CALL IT INSTA-GRAM.

Q: WHAT KIND OF EGG DID THE EVIL CHICKEN LAY?

A: A DEVILED EGG.

Q: WHAT DID THE DRYER SAY TO THE BORING DUVET COVER THAT JUST GOT OUT OF THE WASHER?

A: DON'T BE SUCH A WET BLANKET.

Q: WHAT'S A WRITER'S FAVORITE TRAIN STATION?

A: PENN STATION.

---◇◇---

Q: WHAT'S IT CALLED WHEN KITTENS GET STUCK IN A TREE?

A: A CAT-ASTROPHE.

---◇◇---

Q: WHAT IS MARCO'S FAVORITE CLOTHING STORE?

A: POLO.

---◇◇---

Q: WHAT DID THE BAKER SAY WHEN SHE WON AN AWARD?

A: IT WAS A PIECE OF CAKE!

Q: HOW DO FROGS INVEST THEIR MONEY?

A: THEY USE A STOCK CROAKER.

Q: HOW WAS THE HANDSOME RUNNER DESCRIBED?

A: DASHING.

Q: WHY DID THE OREO GO TO THE DENTIST?

A: HE LOST HIS FILLING.

Q: WHY DON'T PHONES EVER GO HUNGRY?

A: THEY HAVE PLENTY OF APPS TO CHOOSE FROM.

DID YOU HEAR ABOUT THE GUY WHO DRANK INVISIBLE INK?

HE'S AT THE HOSPITAL WAITING TO BE SEEN.

Q: WHY DID THE COMPUTER CATCH A COLD?

A: IT LEFT A WINDOW OPEN.

Q: WHAT KIND OF BIRD WORKS ON A CONSTRUCTION SITE?

A: A CRANE.

Q: WHAT DO YOU CALL A CAN OPENER THAT DOESN'T WORK?

A: A CAN'T OPENER.

Q: DO MASCARA AND LIPSTICK EVER ARGUE?

A: SURE, BUT THEN THEY MAKEUP.

Q: HOW DO YOU GET A GOOD PRICE ON A SLED?

A: YOU HAVE TOBOGGAN.

Q: WHAT DO YOU CALL TWO OCTOPUSES THAT LOOK THE SAME?

A: ITENTICLE.

5/4 OF PEOPLE ADMIT THAT THEY'RE REALLY BAD AT FRACTIONS.

Q: WHAT KIND OF COFFEE DOES A VAMPIRE DRINK?

A: DE-COFFIN-ATED.

Q: AIR USED TO BE FREE AT THE GAS STATION. NOW IT'S $1.50. YOU KNOW WHY?

A: INFLATION.

Q: WHAT DO YOU CALL IT WHEN A LAWYER TAKES A TEST EARLY IN THE MORNING?

A: A BREAKFAST BAR.

Q: WHAT DID THE FISHERMAN SAY TO THE MAGICIAN?

A: PICK A COD, ANY COD!

Q: HOW DO YOU GET YOUR PHONE DRUNK?

A: GIVE IT SCREENSHOTS.

Q: WHAT DID IS SERVED HOT BUT ALWAYS COLD?

A: CHILI.

Q: WHAT GETS WETTER THE MORE IT DRIES?

A: A TOWEL!

Q: WHY DIDN'T THE SUN GO TO COLLEGE?

A: IT ALREADY HAD A MILLION DEGREES.

Q: WHAT DO YOU CALL A HOT DOG ON WHEELS?

A: FAST FOOD!

Q: WHERE DO YOUNG TREES GO TO LEARN?

A: ELEMENTREE SCHOOL.

Q: WHAT DID THE VET SAY TO THE CAT?

A: HOW ARE YOU FELINE?

Q: HOW MUCH DOES IT COST SANTA TO PARK HIS SLEIGH?

A: NOTHING, IT'S ON THE HOUSE.

Q: WHAT DID ONE WALL SAY TO THE OTHER?

A: I'LL MEET YOU AT THE CORNER.

DID YOU HEAR ABOUT THE RESTAURANT ON THE MOON?

GREAT FOOD, NO ATMOSPHERE.

I THOUGHT ABOUT GOING ON AN ALL-ALMOND DIET.

BUT THAT'S JUST NUTS!

A FURNITURE STORE KEEPS CALLING ME.

ALL I WANTED WAS ONE NIGHTSTAND.

I SLEPT LIKE A LOG LAST NIGHT.

WOKE UP IN THE FIREPLACE!

DID YOU HEAR ABOUT THE RED AND BLUE SHIPS THAT COLLIDED?

ALL THE SAILORS WERE MAROONED.

Q: WHY DID THE INVISIBLE MAN TURN DOWN THE JOB OFFER?

A: HE COULDN'T SEE HIMSELF DOING IT.

Q: HOW CAN YOU TELL IF A TREE IS A DOGWOOD TREE?

A: BY ITS BARK.

MOST PEOPLE ARE SHOCKED WHEN THEY FIND OUT HOW BAD OF AN ELECTRICIAN I AM.

Q: WHAT DID ONE EYE SAY TO THE OTHER EYE?

A: BETWEEN YOU AND ME, SOMETHING SMELLS.

Q: WHAT MUSICAL INSTRUMENT IS FOUND IN THE BATHROOM?

A: A TUBA TOOTHPASTE.

Q: WHAT IS THE BEST CHRISTMAS PRESENT EVER?

A: A BROKEN DRUM, YOU CAN'T BEAT IT!

Q: WHY SHOULD YOU WEAR 2 PANTS WHEN YOU GOLF?

A: IN CASE YOU GET A HOLE-IN-ONE!

Q: WHAT'S THE KING OF ALL SCHOOL SUPPLIES?

A: THE RULER.

Q: WHY ARE CATS BAD STORYTELLERS?

A: BECAUSE THEY ONLY HAVE ONE TALE.

Q: WHERE DO FROGS DEPOSIT THEIR MONEY?

A: IN A RIVER BANK.

Q: HOW DID THE POLICE FINALLY STOP THE PAINT THIEF?

A: THEY CAUGHT HIM RED HANDED.

◆◆

Q: WHAT STATE DO CRAYONS GO TO ON VACATION?

A: COLOR-ADO.

◆◆

Q: WHAT'S THE DIFFERENCE BETWEEN A GUITAR AND A FISH?

A: YOU CAN'T TUNA FISH.

◆◆

Q: WHY DID THE WATCH GO ON VACATION?

A: IT NEEDED TO UNWIND.

Q: WHAT DO YOU CALL A BABY MONKEY?

A: A CHIMP OFF THE OLD BLOCK.

Q: WHAT DO YOU CALL SPIDERS WHO JUST GOT MARRIED?

A: NEWLY-WEBS.

Q: WHY DOES THE CLOCK BREAK WHEN IT GETS HUNGRY?

A: IT GOES BACK FOUR SECONDS!

Q: HOW WELL DID I HANG UP THAT PICTURE?

A: I NAILED IT.

Q: WHAT DO YOU CALL A BOOMERANG THAT DOESN'T COME BACK?

A: A STICK.

HAVE YOU HEARD ABOUT THE CHOCOLATE RECORD PLAYER?

IT SOUNDS PRETTY SWEET.

Q: WHAT CONCERT COSTS JUST 45 CENTS?

A: 50 CENT FEATURING NICKELBACK.

Q: WHY CAN'T YOU TRUST ANYTHING BALLOONS SAY?

A: THEY'RE FULL OF HOT AIR.

Q: WHERE DO SHARKS GO ON VACATION?

A: FINLAND!

A: WHAT DO YOU CALL A DINOSAUR WITH A EXTENSIVE VOCABULARY?

A: A THESAURUS.

Q: WHAT DID THE MAN SAY TO THE WALL?

A: ONE MORE CRACK LIKE THAT AND I'LL PLASTER YOU.

Q: DID YOU HEAR THE JOKE ABOUT THE ROOF?

A: NEVER MIND, IT'S OVER YOUR HEAD.

Q: HOW DO YOU LIFT AN ELEPHANT WITH ONE HAND?

A: YOU CAN'T, ELEPHANT ONLY HAVE FEET.

Q: HOW DID BENJAMIN FRANKLIN FEEL WHEN HE DISCOVERED ELECTRICITY?

A: HE WAS SHOCKED.

Q: WHICH IS THE WORST SPORT TO PLAY?

A: BAD-MINTON.

Q: WHY WAS THE HORSE SO HAPPY?

A: BECAUSE HE LIVED IN A STABLE ENVIRONMENT.

Q: WHAT DO RABBITS NEED AFTER GETTING CAUGHT IN THE RAIN?

A: A HARE DRYER!

Q: WHY DID THE COACH PUT THE FROG IN THE OUTFIELD?

A: HE'S REALLY GOOD AT CATCHING FLIES.

Q: WHAT DO YOU CALL A WIZARD WHO'S GOOD WITH CERAMICS?

A: HARRY POTTERY.

Q: WHAT HAS A SPINE BUT NO BONES?

A: A BOOK.

I TOLD MY WIFE SHE SHOULD EMBRACE HER MISTAKES.

SHE GAVE ME A HUG.

Q: HOW DOES A MAN ON THE MOON CUT HIS HAIR?

A: ECLIPSE IT.

Q: I FOUND A WOODEN SHOE IN MY TOILET TODAY.

A: IT WAS CLOGGED.

Q: WHAT IS A CALENDAR'S FAVORITE FOOD?

A: DATES.

MY DOCTOR TOLD ME I WAS GOING DEAF.

THE NEWS WAS HARD FOR ME TO HEAR.

Q: WHAT DO YOU CALL A DONKEY WITH ONLY THREE LEGS?

A: A WONKEY.

Q: HOW DO YOU TELL THE DIFFERENCE BETWEEN A BULL AND A MILK COW?

A: IT IS EITHER ONE OR THE UTTER.

Q: WHAT DO YOU CALL A POTATO WEARING GLASSES?

116

A: A SPEC-TATER.

I GOT A HEN TO REGULARLY COUNT HER OWN EGGS.

SHE'S A REAL MATHAMACHICKEN.

―――――◇◇―――――

Q: WHAT HAPPENS WHEN YOU GO TO THE BATHROOM IN FRANCE?

A: EUROPEAN.

―――――◇◇―――――

Q: WHAT DO YOU CALL A FISH WEARING A BOW TIE?

A: SOFISHTICATED.

―――――◇◇―――――

Q: WHAT ROCK GROUP HAS FOUR MEN THAT DON'T SING?

A: MOUNT RUSHMORE.

Q: WHAT LOOKS LIKE HALF AN APPLE?

A: THE OTHER HALF.

Q: HOW CAN YOU TELL BY SOMEONE'S HOME IF THEY'RE A HIGHWAY ROBBER?

A: ALL THE SIGNS WILL BE THERE.

Q: WHAT BOARD GAME IS POPULAR IN PRAGUE?

A: CZECHERS.

Q: WHAT RHYMES WITH BOO AND STINKS?

A: YOU.

Q: HOW DO GHOSTS STAY IN SHAPE?

A: THEY EXORCISE.

Q: HOW DOES DARTH VADER LIKE HIS BAGELS?

A: ON THE DARK SIDE.

Q: DID YOU HEAR ABOUT THE ICE CREAM TRUCK ACCIDENT?

A: IT CRASHED ON A ROCKY ROAD.

Q: WHAT DO SANTA'S ELVES LISTEN TO AS THEY WORK?

A: WRAP MUSIC.

DID YOU HEAR ABOUT THE GUY WHO INVENTED LIFESAVERS?

THEY SAY HE MADE A MINT.

Q: WHAT DO YOU CALL A SHOE MADE OF A BANANA?

A: A SLIPPER.

Q: WHAT KIND OF MUSIC DID THE PILGRIMS LISTEN TO?

A: PLYMOUTH ROCK.

Q: WHY DO DOGS FLOAT IN WATER?

A: BECAUSE THEY ARE GOOD BUOYS.

THEY DON'T WATCH THE FLINTSTONES IN DUBAI.

BUT ABU DHABI DO.

Q: WHY DO VAMPIRES SEEM SICK?

A: THEY'RE ALWAYS COFFIN.

Q: WHERE DO DADS STORE THEIR BEST DAD JOKES?

A: IN THEIR DAD-A-BASE!

Q: WHAT DO YOU SAY TO COMFORT THE GRAMMAR POLICE?

A: THEY'RE, THEIR, THERE...

Q: WHAT DID THE CELERY SAY TO THE VEGETABLE DIP?

A: I'M STALKING YOU.

Q: WHAT TEN LETTER WORD STARTS WITH GAS?

A: AUTOMOBILE.

Q: WHAT HAPPENS IF YOU SWALLOW A DICTIONARY?

A: YOU'LL GET THESAURUS THROAT EVER.

Q: WHAT'S GREEN AND SLIMY AND HAS ITS OWN TALK SHOW?

A: OKRA WINFREY.

Q: WHAT DID THE GINGERBREAD MAN PUT ON HIS BED?

A: A COOKIE SHEET.

I USED TO RUN A DATING SERVICE FOR CHICKENS BUT I WAS STRUGGLING TO MAKE HENS MEET.

Q: WHAT DO YOU CALL A DICTIONARY ON DRUGS?

A: HIGH DEFINITION!

Q: WHY DO MERMAIDS WEAR SEASHELLS?

A: BECAUSE D-SHELLS ARE TOO BIG.

Q: WHAT DO YOU CALL AN INDECISIVE INSECT?

A: A MAY-BEE.

Q: WHAT DO YOU DO WITH DEAD CHEMISTS?

A: BARIUM.

Q: WHAT IS A TREE'S FAVORITE SODA?

A: ROOT BEER.

Q: WHAT DO YOU CALL A WEIGHT-LOSS MANTRA?

A: FAT CHANTS.

Q: DID YOU HEAR ABOUT THE NEW DATING SERVICE IN PRAGUE?

A: IT'S CALLED CZECH-MATE.

Q: WHAT DO YOU CALL AN UNPREDICTABLE CAMERA?

A: A LOOSE CANON.

Q: WHAT DESSERT IS BEST FOR EATING IN BED?

A: A SHEET CAKE.

Q: WHY DID THE MORMON CROSS THE ROAD?

A: TO GET TO THE OTHER BRIDE.

Q: WHAT DO THEY CALL MILEY CYRUS IN EUROPE?

A: KILOMETRY CYRUS.

Q: DAD, ARE WE PYROMANIACS?

A: YES, WE ARSON.

Q: WHY DID SATAN GO TO THE GYM?

A: TO WORK ON HIS 666 PACK.

Q: WHO IS INDIA'S FAVORITE BASKETBALL PLAYER?

A: STEPH CURRY.

Q: WHAT KIND OF MATH DO TREES LOVE?

A: TWIGONOMETRY.

Q: WHAT DID ONE DORITOS FARMER SAY TO THE OTHER?

A: COOL RANCH!

Q: WHAT DOES A THESAURUS EAT FOR BREAKFAST?

A: A SYNONYM ROLL.

Q: WHAT WAS THE NAME OF THE ORIGINAL BOY BAND?

A: THE BACH BOYS.

Q: WHY DON'T PIRATES SHOWER BEFORE WALKING THE PLANK?

A: BECAUSE THEY'LL JUST WASH UP ON SHORE LATER.

Q: WHY IS COLD WATER SO INSECURE?

A: BECAUSE IT'S NEVER CALLED HOT.

Q: WHAT DOES ROCKIN' ROBIN DO WHEN SHE'S BORED?

A: TWEET.

Q: HOW DOES A DYSLEXIC POET WRITE?

A: INVERSE.

Q: WHAT'S A CRAFTY DANCER'S FAVORITE HOBBY?

A: CUTTING A RUG.

Q: WHAT DID THE TWO PIECES OF BREAD SAY ON THEIR WEDDING DAY?

A: IT WAS LOAF AT FIRST SIGHT.

Q: WHAT DID THE ACCOUNTANT SAY WHILE AUDITING A DOCUMENT?

A: THIS IS TAXING.

Q: WHY DO ZOMBIES EAT BRAINS?

A: FOOD FOR THOUGHT.

Q: WHAT DO YOU CALL SOMEONE WHO WON'T STICK TO A DIET?

A: A DESSERTER.

IF THE EARLY BIRD GETS THE WORM,

I'LL SLEEP IN UNTIL THERE'S PANCAKES.

Q: WHY DID WALDO GO TO THERAPY?

A: BECAUSE HE NEEDED TO FIND HIMSELF.

Q: WHY WERE THE UTENSILS STUCK TOGETHER?

A: THEY WERE SPOONING.

Q: WHAT IS A SCARECROW'S FAVORITE FRUIT?

A: STRAW-BERRIES.

SINGING IN THE SHOWER IS FUN UNTIL YOU GET SOAP IN YOUR MOUTH.

THEN IT BECOMES A SOAP OPERA.

Q: WHY WERE SPECTATORS CONFUSED BY THE KOALA'S SELF-PORTRAIT?

A: IT WAS A BEAR.

Q: WHAT'S THE MOST PATRIOTIC SPORT?

A: FLAG FOOTBALL.

Q: WHY DID THE ENVELOPE TAKE SO LONG TO GET READY?

A: IT HAD TO GET ADDRESSED.

Q: WHAT DO YOU CALL A FLIRTATIOUS PHILOSOPHER?

A: SOCRATEASE.

Q: WHAT'S THE DIFFERENCE BETWEEN ROAST BEEF AND PEA SOUP?

A: ANYONE CAN ROAST BEEF.

Q: WHAT'S BLUE AND DOESN'T WEIGH MUCH?

A: LIGHT BLUE

Q: WHY DID STALIN ONLY WRITE IN LOWER CASE?

A: HE WAS AFRAID OF CAPITALISM.

Q: WHAT DO YOU CALL A BABY SHEEP THAT KNOWS KARATE?

A: LAMB CHOP.

Q: WHAT DOES A KARATE MASTER GET REWARDED WITH WHILE DRIVING?

A: A SEAT BELT.

Q: WHAT DO YOU CALL GUYS WHO LOVE MATH?

A: ALGEBROS.

Q: WHY IS TENNIS SUCH A LOUD GAME?

A: BECAUSE EACH PLAYER RAISES A RACKET.

⬦⬦⬦

Q: WHY WOULDN'T THE BAKER EVER SIT DOWN?

A: HE HAD STICKY BUNS.

⬦⬦⬦

Q: WHAT DO YOU CALL A SNAIL WHO FALLS OFF THE TURTLE HE IS RIDING?

A: EX-CARGO.

⬦⬦⬦

Q: WHAT DID THE FLOWERS DO WHEN THE BRIDE WALKED DOWN THE AISLE?

A: THEY ROSE.

Q: WHAT HAPPENS WHEN YOU DRINK A BOTTLE OF BUG REPELLENT?

A: YOUR FLY STOPS WORKING.

Q: WHAT'S A PICKLE'S FAVORITE TV GAME SHOW?

A: LET'S MAKE A DILL.

Q: WHAT DOES AN IRISHMAN GET AFTER EATING ITALIAN FOOD?

A: GAELIC BREATH.

Q: HOW DO COWS SHOP?

A: FROM CATTLE-LOGS.

Q: WHAT HAS EARS BUT CAN'T HEAR?

A: A CORNFIELD.

WHEN THE CANNIBAL SHOWED UP LATE TO THE BUFFET, THEY GAVE HIM THE COLD SHOULDER.

Q: WHAT'S THE FASTEST CELL PHONE PROVIDER?

A: SPRINT.

Q: WHAT DO YOU CALL AN UGLY DINOSAUR?

A: AN EYESAUR.

Q: HOW DID ROMAN BARBERS CUT HAIR?

A: WITH A PAIR OF CAESARS.

Q: WHAT DO DENTISTS CALL X-RAYS?

A: TOOTH PICS.

Q: DID YOU HEAR ABOUT THE DWARF MARRIED COUPLE?

A: THEY STRUGGLED ALL THEIR LIVES TO PUT FOOD ON THE TABLE.

Q: WHAT IS THE PENALTY FOR BIGAMY?

A: TWO MOTHERS-IN-LAW.

Q: WHAT DO YOU CALL IT WHEN STRAWBERRIES PLAY GUITAR?

A: A JAM SESSION.

Q: WHAT MACHINE SHOULD A 65-YEAR-OLD MAN USE TO IMPRESS MUCH YOUNGER WOMEN?

A: AN ATM.

Q: WHAT DO YOU CALL A FIBBING CAT?

A: A LION.

Q: WHAT DO YOU CALL AN OLD MAN WITH GREAT HEARING?

A: DEAF DEFYING.

Q: WHAT DO YOU CALL A SMALL, ROUND GREEN VEGETABLE THAT BREAKS OUT OF PRISON?

A: AN ESCAPE PEA.

Q: WHAT DOES A CONDIMENT WIZARD PERFORM?

A: SAUCERY.

Q: WHY COULDN'T THE TOILET PAPER CROSS THE ROAD?

A: IT GOT STUCK IN A CRACK.

THANK YOU!!!

SERIOUSLY, THANK YOU FOR THE SUPPORT!
I DESIGNED THIS BOOK, WROTE A HANDFUL OF THESE
JOKES, AND PULLED A BUNCH OF MY FAVORITES FROM
20+ OTHER BOOKS IN THE SPRING WHEN I HAD SOME
FREE TIME.

BETWEEN TWO FULL TIME JOBS, 4 DOGS, AND TRYING TO
SAVE ENOUGH MONEY TO BUY AN ICED COFFEE, I FOUND
TIME TO DO THIS AS A HOBBY.

I'VE SPENT MY ENTIRE CAREER IN TELEVISION AS A
MOTION AND GRAPHIC DESIGNER, WORKING WITH THE
BIGGEST NAMES IN MUSIC AND ON THE BIGGEST TV
SHOWS IN HISTORY.

IF YOU'RE NOT HAPPY WITH THE QUALITY, PLEASE
RETURN IT TO AMAZON FOR A REPLACEMENT OR A
REFUND. I HAVE NO CONTROL OVER THE PRINT OR
QUALITY. I'M SELF-PUBLISHED THROUGH AMAZON, SO
IT'S PRINTED ON-DEMAND WHEN YOU PLACE THE
ORDER. I NEVER SEE THE PRODUCT BEFORE THEY'RE
SENT TO CUSTOMERS. SOMETIMES MISTAKES HAPPEN,
AND THAT'S OKAY! BUT IF YOU'RE NOT 100% SATISFIED
WITH THE QUALITY, PLEASE GET A REPLACEMENT.

ALL THE BEST, @BRADLOW

Made in United States
Troutdale, OR
05/30/2024

20231873R00080